the drivers seat

Kaitlyn Lee

THE
OCEAN DEEP

the drivers seat by Kaitlyn Lee

Copyright © 2022 Kaitlyn Lee

All rights reserved. No portion of this book may be reproduced in any form without permission from the publisher, except as permitted by U.S. copyright law.

For permissions contact: Kaitlynjlee22@gmail.com

Cover by Kaitlyn Lee

Illustrations by: Tatiana Marquez-Cordero

ISBN: 978-1-957674-04-9 print
Library of Congress Control Number: 2022909496
Published by The Ocean Deep Publishing

13833 Dumfries Rd, Manassas, VA 20112

Printed in USA

Why do we think super of man but we have to wonder of women- Kim B. Miller

for the party people of 1313

Contents

all for me	1
adventures	2
new	4
nine years old again	5
street signs	8
impasse	10
heros	13
monochrome	14
paper girl	17
dont distract me	18
let me rest	21
her	24
fall again	26
whipers	29
clutter	31
baggage	33
shatter	34
banana	36
my apologies	38

all for me

i don't mind doing things alone
i actually crave it sometimes.
i like to buy myself roses
and take pictures of the sunset
on drives home from chick-fil-a
and edit them to fit my vsco theme.
i buy a new children's book
and read it on the bench at burke lake park
with a thick crocheted blanket i made myself.
i go to museums and libraries
and venture into new forms of art
then dream about them when i get home.
i like to scream Taylor Swift's re-recordings
and not care what the people at the red light beside me think.

it's important to me that i learn to be friends with myself

i walk through target, just to spend money on random sunglasses
i'll never wear
just as an excuse to buy Starbucks when i leave.
i match my sweaters to my shoes and my purse just to go to
    walmart.
and carry a piece of chocolate with me at all times
in case things get *rough*.
i dance in the rain in the middle of the night
to songs from Adele that i have never related to,
but somehow feel good to scream.
i complete paint by number sets of horses
and hang up the prize painting on my wall when done.
i buy coffee way too many times a week.
and realistically my caffeine intake is much higher than i think.
i put together puzzles and get mad when the last piece doesn't fit.
but i do this all for me.

adventures

We used to go on adventures,
Full of hands exploring each other
The curves of your lips and the
Soft spot on your neck
Sometimes my wandering heart remembers,
filled with an ache for those lost paths

But
I keep my eyes ahead
For I am on my own adventure

And that is just as beautiful.

You fall in love with two types of people.

-someone who will decorate your sky with stars
-someone who will teach you how to shine alone.

new

i bought a new car

it smells of lily and honeysuckle
from the flower shaped air freshener
that hangs on my rearview mirror
the only showcase of personality
is from that scent
its clean, has leather seats
and a sunroof too.
it lacks color from the white exterior
but radiates a clean slate.

soon my seats will be filled with crumbs
from cava and chipotle
and memories of late-night drives.
it will be crowded with
people i've never met before
and last-minute drop-offs.
deep conversations
and tragic heartbreaks.

soon it won't be a new car.

nine years old again

her dimples don't appear as they used to
she used to paint her eyelids in bright blue,
and recite every line from Justin Bieber songs
while jumping and dancing on her bed.
she would wear her cheetah and zebra prints,
not caring if they matched or not,
living her life as a crazed nine-year-old girl.
when she looked into her reflection, she would smile.

now sad as her shoulders don't aline with the edges of her hips
whose smile fades with one look at her stretching stomach
the fears of not looking feminine enough
plagued her brain.

her nights turned into swollen eye mornings,
with breakfast forced down her raggedy throat,
Seventeen magazines became her Bible,
every night barfing up her barely touched dinner.

she plasters fake confidence all over herself
to convince the kids not to make fun
of her shark tooth mangled mess of a mouth
if she just smiles big enough
it'll make up for the tree trunk thighs
and bands of stretch marks encircling them.

the retouched faces with the perfect product placement,
told her she wasn't good enough for them
but no matter what concealer you sell her,
it won't be able to erase her personality
because concealer is only supposed to hide pimples
not people

she wouldn't always feel like a fraud in her own body
that no sandpaper tentacles of self-loathing would slither
up her baby-pink skin every time she looked at herself.
there would be a day she doesn't wish to be buried prematurely

the stinging remarks of classmates no longer torment her,
her earbuds will once again blast Justin Bieber
and the fears of having a fresh face won't send her in tears.
a day where she will feel nine years old again.

make me a weak one
make the road ahead crackle
let me break away

street signs

i often wish there were street signs in life

you see, i'm the type of person
who'd rather be told what to do
because at least i wouldn't feel the *failure*
as much,
but, that's not how life works
that's not how you find meaning on an empty beach road
but it's the empty roads that are the safest
i took a trip last summer

                      the brown rock road with towns only meant
                              for passing through,
                                      never staying.
                                the road never *bent-*
        it was stift like the people in the surrounding towns
                            never moving never changing
                              the scenery passed by but
                                    it was all the same-
                        i could see what came for miles
                   but i could see what i left *behind*

returning to my familiar roads i was met with *dis-connection*
roads i could turn and stop and speed through
roads with speed bumps and traffic lights
people yelling at you to run the reds and go as soon as its green
this often feels like my life

i wish my life had street signs
stopping me from getting into crashes
a sign telling me not to enter a friendship that would leave
me heartb r o k e n.
a sign aching red that would tell me to stop
when things aren't going well

a sign telling me to go faster
with faced with a breathless opportunity
the only signs i've seen are ones filled of
self doubt
the ones telling me to proceed with caution
or road work ahead
so instead of putting myself through the bumpy road
i take a different way
signs that warn me of a sharp curve
so i turn around
signs telling me to buckle up
so i stay strapped in the past.
maybe there are street signs in my life
i just choose the ones i want to see

impasse

all and nothing matters
and i'm unsure how to make you understand
that i wish the air in my lungs
was smoke and ash instead.

where the past and present,
youth and adulthood,
are simultaneously blurred before me
and my unstable footing
is making me dizzy.

i wish you would tell me
where to turn next
that my future is sure
that i am still alive
for a clear and direct reason.

where all and nothing matters
and i wish you knew
how comforting
and how alone
it feels to sit here.

why do molds exsit?
when all of us humans just
spend time breaking them.

burn my candle down
let the ashes fly through air
watch me wax away

heroes

i grew up reading stories
about princesses being
saved by their precious princes.
with missing glass slippers and
towers that were too tall,
only a *man* could climb.
i was taught *it* was a fairytale.
being the lady saved from the
dangerous dragon
waiting for a kiss to wake me from my
comfy and cozy coma.
why are we taught *that*?
the concept of depending
on a *man*.
what does he provide me
that i can not provide *myself*?
i can climb down a building
no matter the height.
i'll chemically invent a solution
to an unbreakable coma.
i can buy my own slippers
that aren't made of glass
and walk in them comfortably.

monochrome

i burnt my biology textbook.
i don't want to see how f r a g i l e people are;
i don't want to see their bones laid b a r e
in colorless imitations

can't stand to dissect my humanity like this-
i don't want my feelings to be easily explained
with hormones and diagrams.
i don't want reasons for it- i don't want clear,
or certain answers to any of my questions.

a part of me doesn't even want to capture
all this mess in my own word or photographs-
to dilute any of this color with a poor mockery
of what actual life feels like.
to let my love, and joy, and lust be disrespected so.
even pain; Grief that bonds to you, and anger that drives you-

i cannot bear the thought of life, dismissed.

i'd much rather fall into that void
between the lines of black and white-
no matter of the formless haze
and the lack of clarity in it all.
i would swim in the mud of eternal ambiguity
just to avoid becoming so drained, monochromatic.
and if a life of color means a lack of certainty-
i will saturate, and drown out the absolute.

*a pack of crayons
without my favorite color
a horrible shame.*

paper girl

i call myself a paper girl
born crisp and clean
with straight edges that fit perfectly in a stack of others
lines that are perfectly untouched
open for any and every imaginable thought
but all it took
was one mess up
to crush the veil of innocence into a little ball
make me wrinkled and torn.
tossed into the corner
every last ounce of free space
used and marked over.
never to be back it its original form
because even if i were to be unwrinkled
my edges were now interfered
with swirly reminders from my past,
more frail than before
i was no longer crisp and flat
i was made into my own shape
filled with creases and indents
i no longer sat in a perfect stack
but made my own space
i was flexible now
had room to be myself.

don't distract me

its hard to focus in physics class
when your *carhartt* beanie changes colors in the corner,
a different shade of fog gray or mint every class.
studded rings glisten across fingers that glide through each strand
of shoulder-length hair that falls below.
a laugh is enough to make my eyes switch
from one side of the room to the-other.
i'm getting distracted
by someone that's not for me,

                                                      doesn't fit my *mold*.

tiny earrings along with a nose ring
the smile underneath accentuates
the creases under her caramel-colored eyes
featuring flicks of honey and hazel.
speaking of your eyes,

                                        why do you look over at *me?*

give me a look of interest,
a reason to not take notes.
was it the cascade of jewelry down your ears that drew me in
or the softness of the pink on your *lips?*
the sweet sparkle of lily that brushed my senses
when you passed me to go to your second science class.
or was it your athletic style,
multiple layers of jackets and flannels paired with shades of
   sneakers.
everything is worn for a *reason*, rushed or not
but an effortless nature is always present.
it makes my eyes drift into a dimension where
i taste the flavor of your lip balm and share the jackets you wear.

help pick out new rings so they glisten even stronger,

                                                  across the room at *me*.

take you out for a real time
instead of just sending looks at each other at school events.
but this attraction is just a distraction.

                                                                right?

crisp perfect particles
drift around your pristine place
let me come pop them

let me rest

on the street we ran the red light,
in the backseat of your car
1 am
you're making me think too much
why am i doing this.
my car
parked next to an ihop
my mom thinks i'm eating

                                                                      am i eating?

eating away at the life i could have,
the silver spoon that you wouldn't touch.
the drapes that would be over my window sill
if i hadnt opened them to look for you.
the phone that wouldn't die so quick from late night calls.
my teachers getting mad at me for being late once again
after talking to *you.*

                                                               i am not eating—

i am breathing heavy holding the weight
of your senseless comments
you're beautiful
i am taken into a world where an hour of sleep is sufficient
and leaving me to think about my action is the language provided,
that i'm supposed to be fluent in.
when will i have a b r e a k

                                                                    oh wait

we haven't talked in a month
i find myself driving that street every day
and somehow i still want a manipulator in my way
how could i be so oblivious to the plans
i thought you would be my *breath of fresh air*
you really just polluted my life.

i dont want the cake
i need a different flavor
maybe the ice cream.

her

it's not normally a *her*
that catches my eye in the hall
i'm used to a him or he.
she reads magazines
in her car as the traffic dies down
and works out in her free time.

it's not normally a *her*
that causes me to fall
i'm used to a him or he.
but she swings a tote bag
with baby bunnies on it,
and carries around clusters
of citrine and carnelian in her pocket.

it's not normally a *her*
that causes me to recall
i'm used to a him or he
but she sends my thoughts running
in our government class
and talks about wanting to
raise plants as her kids.

it's not normally a *her*
but she gives me safety and
a space to let my butterflies
release from my stomach.
she paints pictures on picnics
and enjoys getting lost in the woods
trying to find flowers
that match our sun signs.

its not normally a her
but I'm glad it's *her*

fall again

the waterfall of emotions builds in my brain
searches for passageways to my heart.
is my head making these decisions?

> don't text mom
> *just react*
> don't stay at 45
> *speed*
> don't say no to taking her home
> *this is what you've wanted.*

>> it started out silent
>> awkward almost
>> wandering eyes and fidgets with our phones
>> a laugh escapes her mouth
>> the dam has b r o k e n.

>>> Its called: freefall, blasts
>>> filling our gap.
>>> she slides her knee up to her chest
>>> getting *comfortable.*
>>> my eyes leave the road as words leave my
>>>   mouth

>>>> soon she's singing to me.
>>>> a high of confusion yet comfort take
>>>>   over,
>>>> the water is sinking through the
>>>>   valves
>>>> freefalling into my heart

there is no distraction I don't want
her hands holding my arm,
her fingers fondling my phone
her nails glazing through her hair
only 30 more minutes until we're there

    every light stays green
    and the water is now a stream
    the open road is narrowing
    we are supposed to slow to a trickle
    but the dam doesn't *close*
    my cheeks consume all the adrenaline
    as her fingertips
    brush my face
    hydrating the *heat* created between us.

        i come to her street
        and the once crashing waves
        wade back into the abyss
        i start to feel what i will miss

            the door opens and the emotions
            that i felt leave with her
            i am left with nothing
            but the urge to

                        fall

                            again.

come make me nervous,
walk into a empty room
leave me with a smile

wipers

water drips down the windows
it adds to the fog created from the inside
it makes streaks and lines that overlap
why am i focused on that

you reach *your* hand up and draw two dots
a curve follows.
a smile.
you look at me
the ceiling light glistens onto *your* eyes.

                                                                      you look away.

i am that drop on the windshield
i follow every move *you* make to a tee and nothing less
i mirror myself to *you*
interconnect with other people in *your* life to make *you* like
   me.
i listen to *your* spotify playlists
and buy the same hair clips as *you*,
green butterflies with purple carnations.
i use the decorations on *your* jeans and tees
to embellish my room with every bit of *you*.

i wear the jewelry that we made together
hoping someone will ask me about it
so i can flourish in the thought of

                                      telling someone about *you*

i am the first to like *your* instagram posts
and i leave a comment on every one
begging for a reply.

i pay attention to the little things,
your new hair cut, a new magnet on
the back of *your* car, a new song on *your* playlist

                      i even watch the water drip down *your* windows

but *you* are focused on driving
the water drips down the window
i thought *you* wanted to grasp my hand
but *you* just turned *your* windshield wipers on.

clutter

silence somewhere
resonates within
an empty room
the clutter is now clean
and you are set to start again
you wonder why you didn't do it sooner
why you didn't clear your mind
when the clouds loomed
and the laundry built up
and that cycle repeats aligned
but the *change* will always come
and you'll always have to adjust
new mentalities arent an if
but a must.

if as soon as you
push forward, you fall backwards
where do you end up?

baggage

our friendship has turned into a suitcase
on the conveyor belt of an airports baggage claim
that never gets picked up

something unwanted,
forgotten.

this time around
i won't run back to grab it
to drag it along for
another dreadful year,
because all it does
is weigh me down
when all i want
to do is fly.

shatter

you wake up at the
crack of dawn,
you study
you do your homework,
you go to sleep on time,
you meet your friends for lunch
yet, nobody knows what's on your mind.
there is something *seriously* messed up about you
because you dream of your ex at night.
in class, you're thinking of setting your body ablaze,
storms arise, but you still sit by the window
until it threatens to shatter on your *face.*
abstract thoughts, you can never make sense of yourself.
why am i thinking of someone who doesn't think of me?
you end up crying to sleep
mission complete.

banana

i did not have a banana today

it made me feel bad because
i have a banana every day
bananas are full of magnesium
vitamin c and vitamin b-6
its night now
my stomach hurts
my head hurts my shoulders hurt too
i can choose between two things
a) my day is determined by me consuming a banana or not, or
b) the bananas day is determined by whether i eat it or not.

i did not eat the banana

i thought about it and linked all my problems to its absence
my stomach hurts because i haven't eaten anything
my head hurts because i hit it near the door
my shoulders hurt because i didn't sleep on a pillow
i can either blame my unproductivity on the *absence* of the banana
or i can pull my socks up and eat a banana tomorrow.

*let's speak truth. some of
my worse thoughts are based off of
my greatest actions*

my apologies

i'm sorry
i should've been a better daughter.
i should've *picked* you up off the bathroom floor
and made myself dinner that night.

                                                       i'm sorry
                                  for treating you so shitty.
                              for not understanding
                            how *hard* it is for you to be
                                         a *good* parent

i'm sorry
for being a teenager.
that went and turned into an alien
disappeared to another planet,
who *won't* come home
who wont say i love you again until i turn 25.

                                                         i'm sorry
                                          for not hearing you
                                                  cry out.
                                    because a listener needs
                                              a *listener* too.

i'm sorry
for not picking the college *you* wanted
for not living the life you couldnt have
but gave me.
will you still be proud of *me*?

                                                         i'm sorry
                        i know the *grief* was hard to cover up
                      you tried everything to make it seem like
                                          it was nothing

i'm sorry
for not being interested in having kids
and wanting to have a wife
or at least feel comfortable
introducing you to her.

> i should've been more considerate
> i should have told you all of this
> *sooner.*

acknowledgments

"clutter" and "paper girl" were first published in *Siren*
"Monochrome" was first published in *The Megalodon*

"paper girl" that was spoken about in the *Just In Case You Feel The Same* podcast by Alana Beasley

There are many people I would like to recognize in this wonderful process of publishing this book, I would not be here without any of them.

First, my lovely illustrators, Both Tatiana Marquez-Cordero and A. Bowman, the incredible concept I had for this book would not have come to life without the use of their talents.

The classmates and friends that surrounded me during this project. Both inside the Creative writing program and outside of the program. The amount of support and individuality that was given to me throughout my time in the program was outstanding, I will forever charish the lessons learned and memories we all made as a whole. I am so incredibly proud to have been in the presence of each and every one of the people in room 1313. Each and every one of you have taught me amazing things and I would not be the writer or person I am today without spending time with all of you. I can not wait to see what all of you accomplish, no matter how far we all are from each other you will always have my support.

To my amazing creative writing teacher, Ms. Jessica Dyche, I would not be the person I am today without you, you have taught me that its okay to be imperfect and undeniably yourself, that failure is okay as long as you have learned something from it. I also learned that there is always a way to deal with any situation that is thrown at you, and that is by writing poetry, the easiest form of therapy that I never knew would be so vital in my high school years, you taught me to push the boundaries. Most importantly you created the most incredible space for every student to be their own unique self and that is something that every student from

1313 appreciates you for. So thank you for everything I will never forget the time I got to spend in your presence.

My mother, for being so understanding throughout the years I didn't let you read my poetry. I know it was so difficult but you never let if offend you. Thank you for giving me grace in times where all I needed to do was write. I hope you enjoyed seeing what came from those times.

lastly I would like to thank myself, for getting through this outstanding project in one piece and coming out even stronger than I was before.

Kaitlyn Lee is a graduate of the Creative Writing Program from Charles J. Colgan Senior High school Center for fine and performing arts, she is a former Poetry Editor For the school's Literary Journals. Kaitlyn is currently attending Virginia Commonwealth Univeristy. Formor works of hers can be found in *Siren* and *The Megalodon*. Kaitlyn enjoys spending time with her family and her dog Zamboni and taking time outside to enjoy nature.

Printed by BoD"in Norderstedt, Germany